The Big NOISY Book of
Things That Go

DK UK
Senior editor Gill Pitts
Managing editor Laura Gilbert
Managing art editor Diane Peyton Jones
Producer, pre-production Nadine King
Producer Srijana Gurung
Publisher Sarah Larter
Publishing director Sophie Mitchell
Art director Martin Wilson
Consultant and author of new text Phil Hunt

DK India
Editor Ishani Nandi
Assistant editor Anwesha Dutta
Art editors Shipra Jain, Yamini Panwar
Assistant art editor Jaileen Kaur
DTP designers Md Rizwan,
Vijay Kandwal, Bimlesh Tiwary
Managing editor Alka Thakur Hazarika
Senior managing art editor Romi Chakraborty
CTS manager Balwant Singh
Production manager Pankaj Sharma
Jacket designers Kartik Gera, Dheeraj Arora
Picture researcher Nishwan Rasool

Original project editor Caroline Bingham
Original art editor Sara Hill
Senior editor Sheila Hanly

First published in Great Britain in 1994
This revised edition published in 2016 by Dorling Kindersley Limited
80 Strand, London WC2R 0RL

Copyright © 1994, © 2016 Dorling Kindersley Limited
A Penguin Random House Company
10 9 8 7 6 5 4 3 2 1
001-294627-July/2016

A CIP catalogue record for this book is available from the British Library.
ISBN: 978-0-2412-5764-7

Printed and bound in China

A WORLD OF IDEAS:
SEE ALL THERE IS TO KNOW

www.dk.com

Picture credits: The publisher would like to thank the following for their kind permission to reproduce their photographs. (Key: a-above; b-below/bottom; c-centre; f-far; l-left; r-right; t-top) 1 Corbis: Photolibrary. 4 123RF.com: federicofoto (cl); Dmitriy Sladkov (cla). Dorling Kindersley: John Wilkes, Model Exhibition, Telford (tl). 5 Corbis: Photolibrary (cra). Dreamstime.com: Shaiful Rizal Mohd Jaafar (bl). 6 123RF.com: Visions Of America LLC (cr). Dorling Kindersley: The National Cycle Collection (cr). 7 Dorling Kindersley: Nationaal Luchtvaart-Themapark Aviodome (b); R. Florio (cl). Getty Images: Science & Society Picture Library (crb). 8 Dreamstime.com: Zkruger (t). 9 Dreamstime.com: Djidji (cr); Rui Matos (t). 10 123RF.com: Robert Wilson (cl). Dreamstime.com: Konstantinos Moraitis (t). First Waste, Hendon, London (br). 11 Robert Harding Picture Library: Adam Woolfitt (crb). 12 Dorling Kindersley: George and Steven Harmer (tl); The National Motor Museum, Beaulieu (cl). Dreamstime.com: Odecam650 (bl). 13 Corbis: Transtock (b). Dorling Kindersley: Phil Davies (cra); George Manning (cl); Trevor Pope Motorcycles (crb). 14 Dreamstime.com: Ukrid Yenpetch (cr). Robert Harding Picture Library: Ian Griffiths (b). The Image Bank (cl). Zefa (bl). 15 123RF.com: cyoginan (crb); Steve Estvanik (tl). Zefa (tr). 16 Corbis: Adam Jahiel (cla). Dreamstime.com: Johnhill118 (t). The Image Bank (cl). Zefa (cr). 17 Alamy Images: John Elk III (b). Dreamstime.com: Benjamin Rowland (clb). 18 123RF.com: Robert Keenan (cl). Dreamstime.com: Marilyn Barbone (b). 19 123RF.com: Kasto (b). Tony Stone Images: Alastair Black (t). 20 Dorling Kindersley: Igor Dolgov (b). 21 Corbis: Photolibrary (cr). Balloon Base (Bristol - UK) (br). The J. Allan Cash Photolibrary (clb); (bl). 22 Dreamstime.com: Bob Phillips / Digital69 (tl). Rex Shutterstock: (bl). Velocity Inc (tr). 23 Corbis: ALLISON JOYCE / Reuters (cr). Dreamstime.com: Mariusika11 (cra). Getty Images: FABRICE COFFRINI (bl). Rex Shutterstock: Unimedia Images (cl). Volocopter (r). 24 123RF.com: Melinda Nagy (tl); tan4ikk (cr). 25 123RF.com: Alysta (tl); Tomasz Trojanowski (cr). Corbis: Tammy Ljungblad / ZUMA Press (br). Dreamstime.com: Pavel Losevsky (bl); Wuka (tr). 27 Zefa: Orion Press (bl). 28 Caterpillar (cl). Terex Equipment Ltd (tr). 29 123RF.com: Baloncici (c). 30 Dreamstime.com: Vladimir Bryzgin (bl). 31 123RF.com: Dmitriy Sladkov (bl). Dreamstime.com: Rui Matos / Rolmat (cl). Tadano-Faun (b). David MacKrill Engineering Ltd (cr). 32 123RF.com: claudiodivizia (t). Corbis: Robert Garvey (c). 33 Dorling Kindersley: The Fleet Air Arm Museum (b). Getty Images: SVF2 (cla). Innespace Productions Inc. / Seabreacher: (cr). SEADOO/ Seascooter: (tr). 34 123RF.com: Scott Betts (cl); Stepan Popov (cra). The J. Allan Cash Photolibrary (c). Quadrant (b). 35 Dreamstime.com: Cobia (tl); Photodynamx (cl). Quadrant (t). 36 123RF.com: federicofoto (cr). 37 Alamy Images: IAN MARLOW (tr). The Aviation Picture Library: Austin J. Brown (cl). Oshkosh Truck Corporation (c). 38 123RF.com: Ed Aldridge (cl); Ekasit Wangprasert (tl). Dreamstime.com: Zero Motorcycle (cra). 39 Alamy Images: Business (cr). Corbis: Car Culture (clb); Arctic-Images (br). Getty Images: Scott Barbour (cl). Solar Impulse: (c). 40 123RF.com: Gunter Nezhoda (t). Pete Biro (cl). 41 123RF.com: gors4730 (tr). Corbis: Duomo (bl). 42 Courtesy AgustaWestland: (cr). Dorling Kindersley: The National Railway Museum, York (t). 43 Alamy Images: Erik Tham (c). Corbis: Reuters (t). Dreamstime.com: Evren Kalinbacak (cr). Getty Images: CATRINUS VAN DER VEEN / AFP (clb); Jonathan Torgovnik (br). 44 Dorling Kindersley: John Wilkes, Model Exhibition, Telford (cra). Rex Shutterstock: Geoffrey Robinson (c). Terex Equipment Ltd (tl). 45 Corbis: Kieran Doherty / Reuters (t). NASA (clb) 46 Corbis: Scott Andrews / Science Faction (tc). NASA: Johnson Space Center (r); (bl). 47 Johns Hopkins University Applied Physics Laboratory / Southwest Research Institute. NASA: (br); JPL / Cornell University (cr). SpaceX (r). U.S. Air Force (cla). Dorling Kindersley would also like to thank: Action Vehicles at Shepperton Studios, Middlesex; AirBourne Aviation at Popham Airfield, Nr Basingstoke; Benford Ltd, Warwick; Brands Hatch; Case International; Caterpillar Inc.; G P Edwards; Fairooks Airport Ltd; FLS Aerospace at London Stansted Airport; Gilmar Motor Engineers, Mark Goss; Griffiths Tucker, Liss, Hampshire; Hoverspeed, Dover; JCB; Johnston Engineering Ltd, Dorking, Surrey; Red Watch at Lambeth Fire Station, London; Lasham Gliding, Alton, Hampshire; John McCluskey; New Holland Ford Ltd; P.J.S. (Agricultural Services) Ltd, Newbury; Harbour Manager's Office at the Port of Dover; S.E.C. Fire Protection Ltd at Shepperton Studios; White Watch at Soho Fire Station, London; Blue and Green Watch at London Stansted Airport Fire Service; Ian Vickerstaff at Terex Equipment Ltd, Motherwell, Scotland.

The Big NOISY Book of
Things That Go

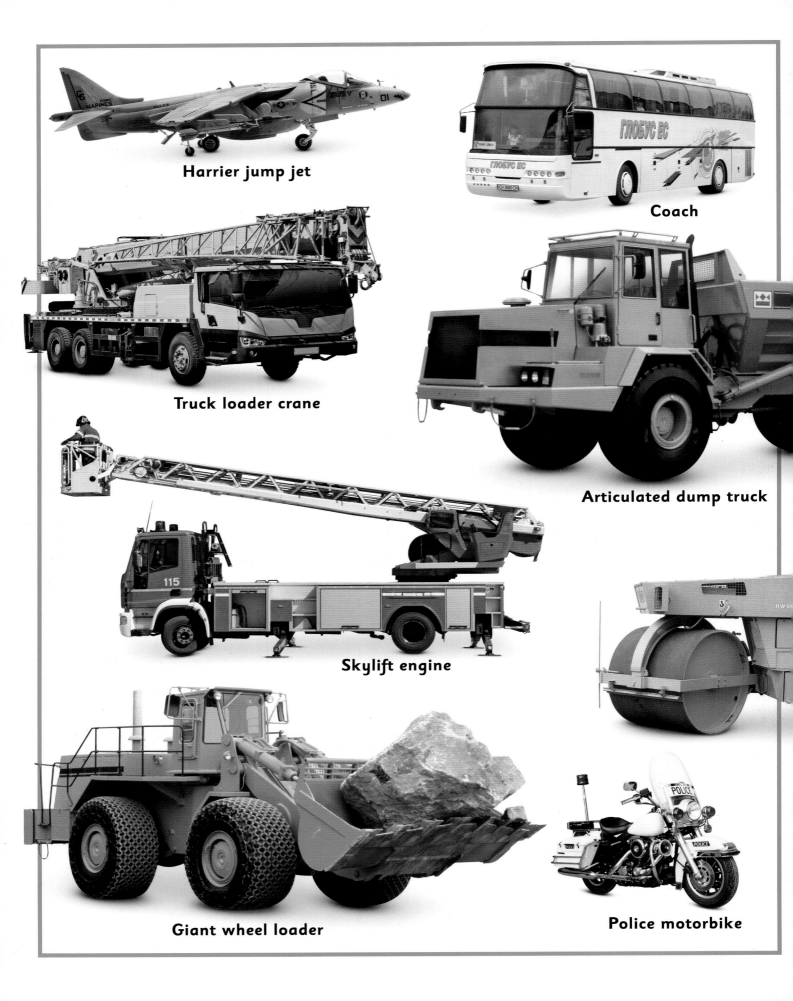

Harrier jump jet

Coach

Truck loader crane

Articulated dump truck

Skylift engine

Giant wheel loader

Police motorbike

Contents

Hot air balloon

Multipurpose truck

Bicycle

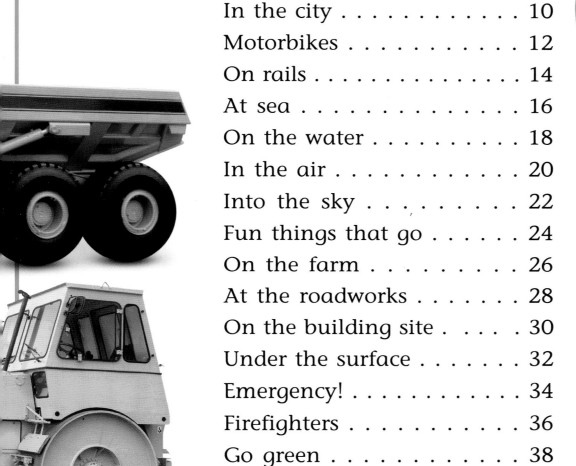

Roller

Racing car

Gondola

Early vehicles

Canoe

For thousands of years, people have used wooden canoes like this to travel on water. Wooden paddles helped them to move and steer.

Skin made of birch tree bark

Driver sits or stands in here

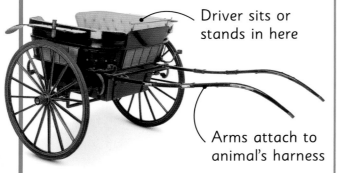

Arms attach to animal's harness

Cart

Carts are simple, two-wheeled vehicles that can be pulled by animals such as horses, donkeys, and oxen. They can carry up to four people at a time.

Penny-farthing

Riders of this very early type of bicycle had to sit above a very large front wheel. They had to take care not to fall off as it was hard to balance.

Leather saddle

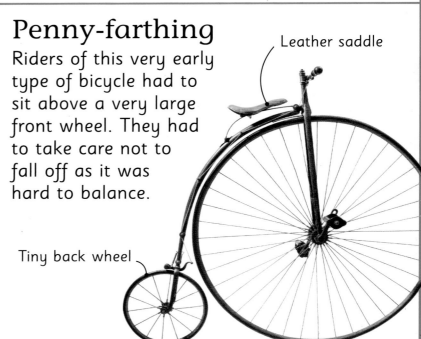

Tiny back wheel

Stagecoach

Before motorized vehicles, stagecoaches were the buses of the day. As well as carrying passengers, these covered, horse-drawn wagons would also transport mail.

Stage driver

Space for luggage

Daimler "Riding Car"

Built in 1885, this two-wheeled machine is one of the world's first ever motorcycles. It could reach a top speed of 11 kph (7 mph).

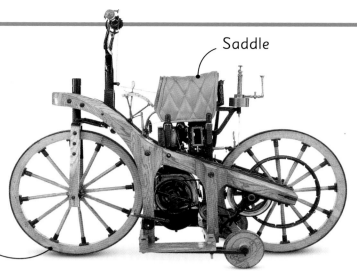

Saddle

Metal rim on wooden wheel

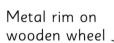

Ford Model T

In 1908, the Ford Model T became the first car that was cheap enough for ordinary people to buy. More than 16 million were made.

Wright Flyer

In 1903, the Wright Flyer became the first powered aircraft to make a successful flight. It was airborne for just 3 seconds.

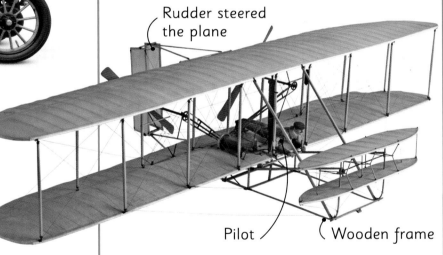

Rudder steered the plane

Pilot

Wooden frame

Passenger airship

In the 1920s and 1930s, airships like this Graf Zeppelin transported passengers around the world. They travelled in cabins fitted to a "gondola" at the front of the craft.

The body of this airship was filled with hydrogen gas

GRAF ZEPPELIN   D-LZ 127

Gondola

On the road

Car transporter

A car transporter can carry many cars at one time. This one is carrying estates, saloons, and other types of car.

Motor caravan

Some people go on holiday in motor caravans. Inside there are beds, a cooker, and a toilet.

Handlebars

Motorbike

Motorbikes have two wheels. The rider steers with the handlebars.

Sports car

A sports car has a powerful engine. Its long, low shape helps it to zoom along at high speeds.

Coach

Coaches carry people on long journeys. This coach has special lockers for bags and rows of comfortable seats.

Lockers

Estate car

An estate car has room for a driver, four passengers, and all their bags. Luggage is stored in the large rear section.

Tanker

Tankers carry liquids in a strong metal tank. This tanker is full of milk that has been collected from a farm.

Metal tank

Pick-up truck

A pick-up truck has a flat, open back. It is useful for carrying small loads.

Boot

Engine

Saloon car

A saloon is a large, comfortable car with four doors. There is space in the boot for luggage.

Transport lorry

Transport lorries carry all sorts of goods. The driver has a special sleeping bunk to use on long journeys.

Sleeping bunk in the back of the cab

In the city

Back door

Hatchback

This car has five doors. The fifth door is at the back. Hatchbacks are popular cars in cities because they are small and easy to park.

Delivery van

Delivery vans carry goods to shops and to people's homes. A sliding side door makes it easy to load up the back of the van.

Side door

Bus

People use buses to go to school or work, and to visit other places. A bus collects its passengers at a bus stop.

Rubbish collection lorry

Rubbish is often collected in lorries like this. Bags of rubbish are crunched up in the back of the lorry.

Bicycle

Riding a bicycle is a quick way of getting around the city. Have you ever ridden a bicycle?

Saddle

Pedal

Rubble container

Water tank

Hose

Road sweeper

A road sweeper has a big hose to suck up dirt and rubble. It is a bit like an enormous vacuum cleaner, but the road sweeper's hose is wide enough to suck up a brick!

Stretch limousine

A stretch limousine is as long as two hatchbacks put together. Some limousines have a television in the back.

"For hire" light

YELLOW CAB

3381 305 444- 4444

Be Your Own Boss
DRIVERS WANTED
444-4444

Taxi

People hire taxis to take them wherever they like in a city. This taxi is from New York City in the USA.

Rickshaw

In some countries, rickshaws are used as taxis to carry people over short distances.

Removal van

A removal van carries furniture when people move to a new home. The van is big enough to carry a whole houseful of furniture.

Motorbikes

Springs

Headlamp

Vintage motorbike

This British Royal Enfield motorbike was built in 1936. Springs under the large saddle made the ride more comfortable.

Early racing bike

In the 1920s, racing motorcycles like this Harley-Davidson raced on dirt roads, wooden tracks, and even hills.

Spare wheel

Scooter

Scooters, such as this 1950s Lambretta, can be recognized by their small wheels. Two seats mean a passenger could sit behind the driver.

Motorbike with sidecar

Some motorbikes can be attached to a sidecar to carry passengers. Some sidecars are open-air, while others are covered.

Open-air sidecar

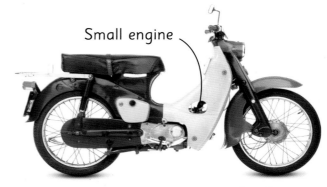

Small engine

Commuter motorbike

The Honda C50 Super Cub is the world's most popular motorcycle. It has a small engine and is easy to ride.

Pannier, or side bag, for carrying radio

Military motorbike

This Harley-Davidson WLA was used by the US Army in World War II. It was a strong and reliable motorcycle.

Large racing exhaust

Superbike

Superbikes are special racing bikes that can travel incredibly fast. This Kawasaki Ninja can reach nearly 300 kph (186 mph).

Touring bike

Touring motorbikes, such as this BMW R 1200 RT, are designed to give riders a comfortable journey over very long distances.

Storage box

Trials bike

With its knobbly tyres, a trials bike is made for racing up muddy tracks and down rocky slopes.

Deep grooves in tyres

Chopper bike

Some riders like to change their bikes by adding long forks, fancy wheels, and special paintwork.

High handlebars

Custom paintwork

Fork connects the front wheel to the frame

13

On rails

Steam train

Trains are pulled by engines. A steam engine driver shovels coal into a fire to heat water. The hot water turns into steam, which powers the engine and turns the wheels.

Wagon contains coal and water

Electric tram

Trams are like buses, but they run on rails along city streets.

Diesel locomotive

This train's engine is powerful. It usually pulls up to 12 carriages along the tracks.

Snow plough train

Snow plough trains use large propellers to blow away snow that has piled up on the rails.

Monorail train

Monorails run on one rail. They are used to carry people over short distances.

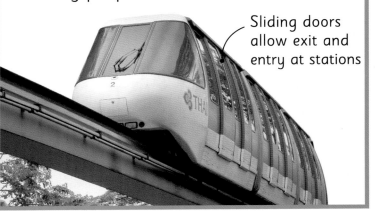

Sliding doors allow exit and entry at stations

Underground train

Underground trains, such as this one in New York, speed along tunnels built under the city's streets.

Rack and pinion train

The rack and pinion train can travel up and down steep hills. It has a toothy wheel that slots into a special rail, like a cog in a machine.

Driver's cab

Shunter

A shunter pushes carriages and goods wagons around a railway yard. It needs a powerful engine.

These buffers are used to push carriages

Maglev train

The Shanghai magnetic levitation train in China travels at very high speeds without touching the rails. Magnets lift and move the train forwards.

Breakdown train

A breakdown train carries a giant crane. If a carriage comes off the rails, the crane lifts it back into position.

The train is controlled from this cab

CRANE RUNNER

At sea

Catamaran

A catamaran has two hulls. These help it to cut quickly through the waves, but make it slower to turn than single-hulled boats.

Hull

Outrigger canoe

A wooden float, or outrigger, makes this sailing boat very steady. In some countries, outrigger canoes are used for fishing.

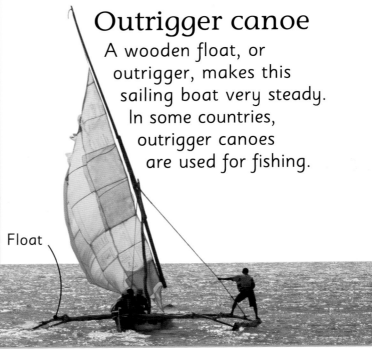

Float

Sub-aqua craft

Sub-aqua craft are used to explore the seabed. They need powerful lamps to light the way.

Tug

A tug uses steel ropes to pull big ships into port. It can also push a ship into position using its back, or stern. This tug has a big tyre on its stern to protect it when it bumps into other boats.

The tug is steered from this room, which is called the bridge

Tyre

Container ship

A container ship carries goods in huge metal crates called containers.

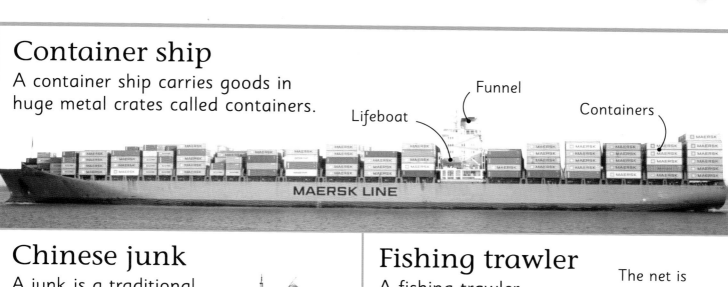

Lifeboat

Funnel

Containers

MAERSK LINE

Chinese junk

A junk is a traditional Chinese sailing ship. It has a wide, flat bottom.

Bamboo sticks, or battens, keep the sail stiff

Fishing trawler

A fishing trawler catches fish in a large net. The net is pulled along behind the boat.

The net is fed through this frame

P40

Hovercraft

Two propellers drive the hovercraft forwards

A hovercraft travels over water on a cushion of air. This hovercraft can carry lots of passengers over short distances.

www.hovertravel.com

Ferry

People use ferries for short journeys across the sea. This ferry has a special deck for cars and lorries.

Vehicles are parked on the lower deck

On the water

Handlebars

Jet ski

A jet ski is a bit like a water motorbike. It whizzes over the water at a great speed, bouncing over the waves. The rider steers the jet ski using handlebars.

Paddle steamer

Paddle steamers like this carry people on river trips. The huge paddle wheel turns in the water, pushing the boat forwards.

Paddle wheel

Sailing dinghy

A sailing dinghy is a small yacht that one or two people can sail.

Mast

Mainsail

Motor cruiser

People go on holiday on motor cruisers. On board there is space for them to cook and sleep.

Cabin

Dinghy, or small boat

Three-masted ship

Big sailing ships like this were once used to carry cargo. They are now used as training ships for young sailors.

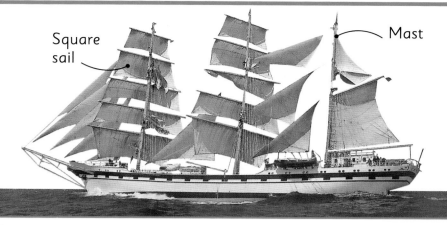

Square sail

Mast

Inflatable

Outboard motor

A trolley is needed if the boat has to be moved on land

An inflatable is made of strong rubber pumped up with air. It has an engine called an outboard motor to make it skim across the water.

Gondola

This gondola carries people on the canals of Venice in Italy. The long oar is used to push the boat through the water.

Oar

Ocean liner

An ocean liner is like a floating hotel. It has cabins, shops, swimming pools, and restaurants.

Swimming pool

In the air

Light aircraft

Light aircraft are used to carry small groups of people on short journeys.

Propeller

Cockpit

Wing

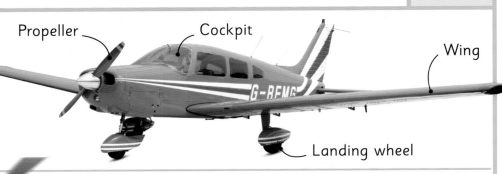

G-REMG

Landing wheel

Rotor shaft

Rotor blade

Helicopter

A helicopter has blades instead of wings. They spin round very fast to lift the helicopter straight up into the air.

Stunt plane

A stunt plane, or aerobat, can loop the loop and even fly upside down!

Wing

G-PITZ

Fabric wing

Propeller

Microlight

The microlight is a very small plane that pilots fly for fun.

Passenger plane

Passenger planes fly people all around the world, on holidays and on business. Have you ever been in a big aeroplane?

Tail fin

The wings of this passenger plane measure 80 m (260 ft) from tip to tip

A380

Own the sky   A380 AIRBUS

Luxury private jet

These luxury aircraft have comfortable recliner-style seats, master bedrooms, and kitchens where chefs can prepare meals.

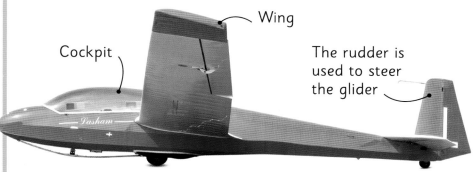

Wing

Cockpit

The rudder is used to steer the glider

Glider

A glider has no engine. It is towed into the sky behind a light aircraft. When the tow cable is released the glider soars through the air.

Flying boat

The lower half of a flying boat is shaped like a boat's hull so that it can land on water. Small floats support its wings.

Float

Seaplane

A seaplane has floats instead of wheels so that it can take off and land on water.

Burners heat the air inside the balloon

Basket

Float

Hot-air balloon

This balloon is filled with hot air, which makes it rise up into the sky. Where do you think the passengers ride?

Into the sky

Frame made of lightweight metal

Pilot swings body to steer

Fabric wing

Hang glider

Like a glider, a hang glider does not have an engine, but uses pockets of rising air to fly.

Kit plane

This aircraft comes in separate parts to build yourself. It takes about 1,500 hours!

Kite surfer

A kite surfer uses a power-kite to catch the wind, which moves the surfboard quickly across the water.

Large kite

Control line

Surfboard

Jet pack

A jet pack releases powerful jets of gas or water that can lift a person high up into the sky. The height, speed, and direction are controlled by the handles.

Volocopter

This is an electric-powered helicopter that can fly two passengers for up to 30 minutes before it needs to be recharged.

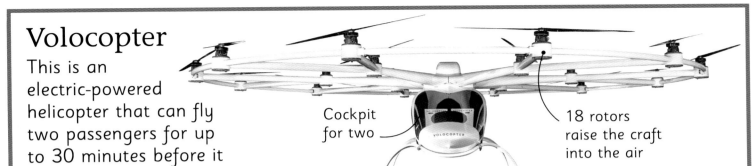

Cockpit for two

18 rotors raise the craft into the air

Super Sky Cycle

This flying tricycle uses a small aircraft engine to power a propeller at the back and a rotor at the top.

Rotor blades are folded when the tricycle is driven on the road

Cockpit

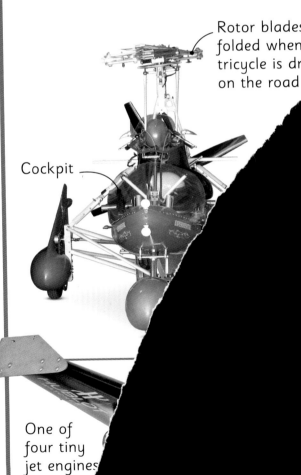

One of four tiny jet engines

Autogyro

An autogryo is like a tiny helicopter

can ca

or

Skis

Clip your boots into the skis, take a chairlift to the top of a snowy mountain then slide down. Whoosh!

Skateboard

With practice you learn some tricks on a board – just fall off!

protector

Wakeboard

Being pulled behind a speedboat on a wakeboard is thrilling, but you will get very wet!

Handle

Wakeboard

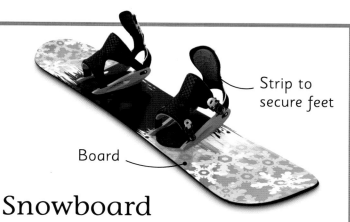

Strip to secure feet

Board

Snowboard

These boards allow you to glide on the snow. You can also do jumps and tricks.

Micro scooter

Both children and adults love whizzing around on micro scooters. They can be folded up and carried under your arm.

Tiny front wheel

Segway

This vehicle is an electric-powered, self-balancing platform with wheels. You lean forwards to move ahead and lean back to slow down.

Handlebar is used to turn left or right

Sensors in the platform keep the rider balanced

Self-balancing board

This two-wheeled, battery-powered board operates just like a Segway, but without a handle.

On the farm

Plough

Tractor

A tractor is a powerful vehicle that is used to pull farm machinery. This tractor is pulling a plough to turn over the earth and bury the weeds.

Tractor with furrow press

Ploughed fields are bumpy. The furrow press flattens the bumps while the power harrow smooths the earth.

Power harrow

Furrow press

Tractor with seed drill

This tractor is planting seeds. The seeds drop into the earth and are covered with soil.

Cab

Hopper contains the seeds

Cab

Tyre

Multipurpose truck

This tough truck is used for different jobs on a farm. It can carry heavy loads and has deep grooves in its tyres to stop it getting stuck in the mud.

Forage harvester

A forage harvester collects mown grass and chops it up. The grass is made into a cattle food called silage.

Driver's cab

Cutting blades to chop mown grass

Farm loader

This farm loader is called a Farm Master. It uses its big shovel to carry grain and cattle food around the farm.

Cab

The arm, or boom, supports the shovel

Shovel

All-terrain vehicle

An all-terrain vehicle, or ATV, can travel over any sort of ground. In Australia, ATVs are often used for rounding up sheep.

Combine harvester

When grain crops such as wheat, corn, and barley are fully grown they are cut, or harvested, with a combine harvester.

The reel pushes crops down into the cutter

Grain tank

Rice harvester

A rice harvester is a cutting machine. It chops down rice plants. These are collected from the field later.

Telescopic handler

Could you lift a bale of hay? It weighs about 20 kg (44 lbs). A telescopic handler can lift 64 bales of hay at a time!

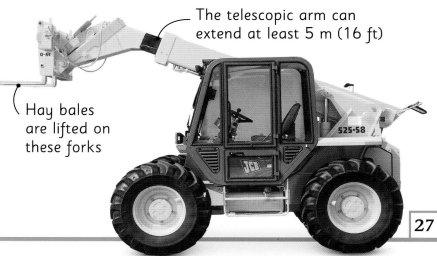

The telescopic arm can extend at least 5 m (16 ft)

Hay bales are lifted on these forks

At the roadworks

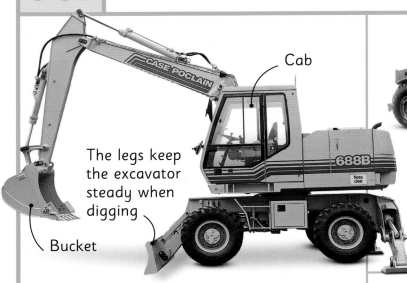

Cab

The legs keep the excavator steady when digging

Bucket

Wheeled excavator
This excavator is like a massive shovel on wheels. Its toothy bucket digs deep trenches.

Blade

Scraper
A scraper uses a sharp blade to cut a path through the soil. This helps to make new roads.

Compactor
A compactor has spiked wheels that squash down the earth to make it flat.

Metal plate clears a path

Grader
A grader has a metal blade that smooths the surface of the earth before a new road is laid.

Blade

Paver
A paver spreads a layer of warm tarmac over the earth once it has been flattened.

Exhaust pipe

A canopy protects the driver from the sun and rain

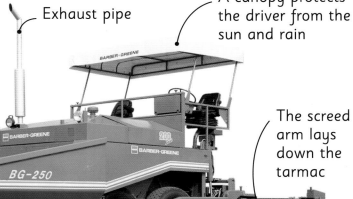

The screed arm lays down the tarmac

The tarmac is tipped into this hopper

Chip spreader

A chip spreader drops a thin layer of small stones over a newly laid surface of a road. The roller then presses these into the tarmac.

Tipper truck

This truck tips out its heavy load, such as sand or gravel, wherever it is needed.

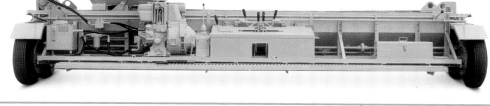

Tipper body

Skid steer

A speedy little skid steer is useful for work where there is not much space.

Bucket

Telescopic boom

A telescopic boom has a long arm. It helps workers reach high up places, such as road lights or bridges.

Arm, or boom

Wheel

Roller

A roller uses its massive wheels to flatten tarmac.

Cab

Roller

On the building site

Bulldozer

Building sites are full of rubble. This bulldozer uses its strong steel blade to push heavy rubble aside.

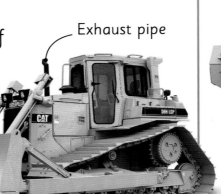

Exhaust pipe

Blade

Metal crawler tracks

Rubble is carried in this skip

Dumper

This tough little dumper carries sand, bricks, or concrete around the site.

Articulated dump truck

An articulated dump truck carries sand, gravel, or stones across the bumpy ground of the building site. The dumper body tips up to empty the load.

An articulated truck bends in the middle

Dumper body

Track excavator

This excavator has a bucket with sharp teeth. These tear into the soil to dig holes.

Arm

The tracks move easily over bumpy ground

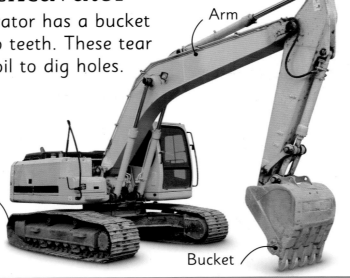

Bucket

Bucket

Wheel loader

A wheel loader's bucket moves up and down, shovelling up earth and stones.

Backhoe loader

A backhoe loader can dig out earth, as well as carry heavy loads.

Arm

Shovel

Bucket

Concrete mixer truck

This concrete mixer truck has a big drum that turns round and round to mix concrete. The drum is emptied through a funnel.

Fork-lift truck

A fork-lift truck is used to move heavy stacks of bricks around a building site.

The prongs slide through or under objects

Skip loader

Skips are used as giant rubbish bins on building sites. Special trucks collect the skips.

Truck loader crane

Crane arm

A truck loader crane has an extending crane arm. On a building site, the crane is used to lift heavy steel bars, called girders, to each new floor of a multistorey building.

Truck cab

Under the surface

London Tube train

Opened in 1863, the London underground railway system – called the "Tube" – is the oldest in the world. On its busiest days it can carry more than 4.8 million people.

Mining truck

Large trucks help underground workers carry and transport heavy material, such as coal, rocks, and soil, in mines.

Hopper, in which up to 60,000 kg (132,270 lbs) of material can be carried

Driver's cab

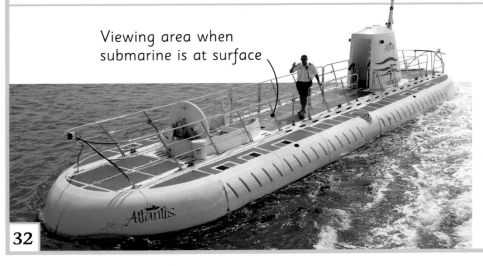

Viewing area when submarine is at surface

Tourist submarine

Submarines such as the Atlantis take passengers 46 m (150 ft) deep into the ocean to see exotic fish, beautiful corals, and old shipwrecks.

Sea scooter

This battery-powered unit can pull a diver through the water at a speed of 5.3 kph (3.3 mph), which is quite fast when travelling underwater.

Entry door for the crew

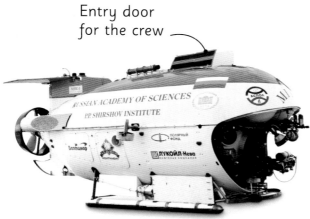

Submersible

The Russian Mir-1 submersible (small submarine) is used to find out about life in the deepest oceans. In 2007, it dived 4,260 m (13,980 ft) down to the seabed under the North Pole.

Diving watercraft

This submersible, called the Seabreacher, is designed to look like a shark. It can dive 1.5 m (5 ft) and travel at a speedy 40 kph (25 mph) while underwater.

Military submarine

With a crew of more than 100 people, large military submarines, such as this one, can stay underwater for many months at a time.

Strong hull made of thick steel

Emergency!

Police motorbike

When police have to get around fast, they can weave through traffic on a motorbike.

Lorry breakdown truck

If a car breaks down, this emergency truck might be able to help to get it moving.

This grill protects the headlights from damage

Flashing lights

Ambulance

Ambulances rush people to hospital. This ambulance has flashing lights to tell other drivers that the ambulance is in a hurry.

Police boat

In many countries of the world, police use boats to speed across the water to help people in trouble.

MIAMI-DADE POLICE

Snow plough

A snow plough has a wide steel blade on the front to shovel snow off the road. It clears the way for cars and lorries.

Winch

Rescue helicopter

Rescue helicopters are used at sea and over mountains. A winch hoists people up into the helicopter.

Lightship

Lightships are anchored near dangerous rocks and sandbanks where a lighthouse cannot be built. The light warns other boats to keep clear.

Light

Police car

This American police car has a loud siren and flashing lights to warn other cars to let the police car pass.

Spectacles

Tow truck

This truck can tow a broken-down car to the garage. The truck lifts the car with a special frame. The frame has spectacles that slot around a car's front wheels.

Lifeboat

A lifeboat heads out to sea in stormy weather to rescue people in trouble. Radar equipment helps the crew to find a boat in distress very quickly.

Radar

50-00!

Firefighters

Airport fire engine

An airport fire engine carries huge amounts of water and foam. The water and foam mixture is squirted onto a fire through the monitor.

Ladder

Monitor

This platform can hold four people

Boom

Skylift engine

A skylift engine can hoist a firefighter up to meet the flames of a fire. A water hose runs up the boom, and the firefighter points it at the flames.

Fire chief's car

This fire car races to the scene of a fire. It gets there before the other fire engines. This gives the chief fire officer time to decide how to put out the fire.

Fire rescue truck

This American truck carries special firefighting equipment such as saws, hammers, and axes. It gives extra support to other fire engines.

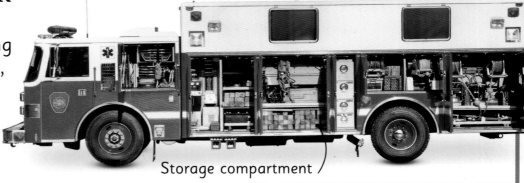

Storage compartment

Water tender engine

A water tender engine carries a tank of water. The hoses are kept rolled up, ready to be used when fighting a fire.

Hoses

Firefighting aircraft

This aircraft is fighting a forest fire. It has special water tanks that it fills by swooping down across the surface of a lake. The water tanks are emptied over the fire.

Rapid intervention vehicle

Rapid intervention vehicles like this are sometimes used at airports. They can reach a fire faster than a big truck.

Monitor   Floodlight

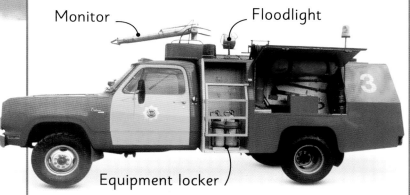

Equipment locker

Articulated fire truck

The front part of this truck is joined to a trailer behind it. The whole vehicle is articulated, which means that it bends in the middle. This helps the driver steer over bumpy or muddy ground.

Trailer

Truck

Go green

Hydrogen cell car
The Toyota Mirai is powered by hydrogen. This means it produces water vapour rather than pollution-causing exhaust gases.

Electric motorbike
This Zero Motorcycles Model S can travel 317 km (197 miles) on a single battery charge.

Aluminium frame

Belt drives the wheel

Hybrid car
Hybrid cars use both a petrol engine and an electric motor. The Toyota Prius was the first model of this type to be produced on a mass scale.

Solar-powered boat
PlanetSolar is the world's largest boat that is powered by energy from the Sun. It was the first such craft to sail completely around the globe.

Energy from solar panels drives the electric motors

TÛRANOR PlanetSolar

CANDINO
SWISS WATCH

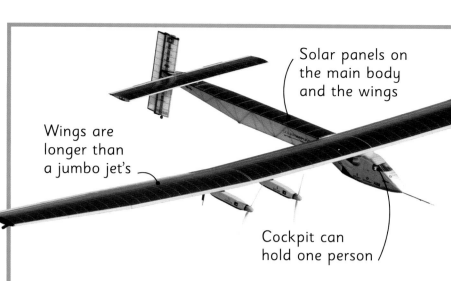

Wings are longer than a jumbo jet's

Solar panels on the main body and the wings

One of four electric motors

Cockpit can hold one person

Solar-powered plane

Solar Impulse 2 flies using solar power. It stores energy during the day so it can fly at night.

Solar car

The Sunswift Solar is the fastest solar-powered car in the world. It can travel at a speed of 132 kph (82 mph).

Solar cells

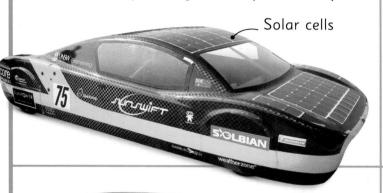

Compressed air car

This French experimental hybrid car has a petrol engine and a motor powered only by compressed air.

Vents take in air to cool the engine

Compressed natural gas car

This Honda has a tank of compressed natural gas in its boot that provides some of the power for the engine.

Hydrogen cell bus

Hydrogen fuel cells generate electricity using hydrogen gas and air. They are used to power buses in some cities.

At the races

Racing car
A racing car hugs the ground as it roars around a race track.

Off-road racer
Off-road racing means a bumpy ride for the driver and passenger. The cars often bounce up into the air!

Go-kart
Go-karts are small racing machines. They are driven round special tracks.

Go-kart racers must wear a helmet

Small tyres

Powerboat
A powerboat has a long, narrow shape and a powerful engine. This helps it to slice through the water at top speed.

Hull

Motocross bike
Motocross bikes race over rocky and muddy ground, and up steep hills.

Racing motorbike

This motorbike races at high speed on a racing track. What differences can you see between this motorbike and a motocross bike?

Sidecar racer

A sidecar racer takes two people. They lean from side to side to balance the bike.

Racing yacht

This racing yacht has a big crew. The crew pull on ropes called sheets to change the position of the sails. The sails catch the wind and make the yacht speed across the water.

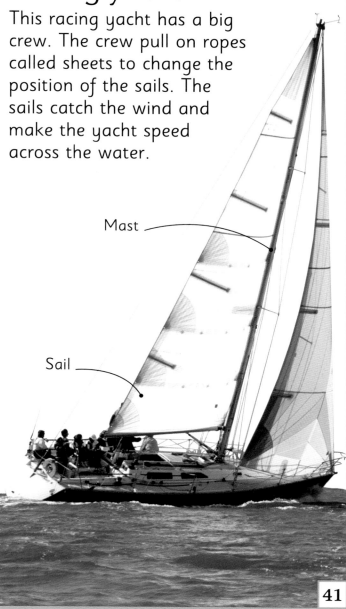

Mast

Sail

Massive tyre

Monster truck

These heavy vehicles can be more than 3 m (10 ft) tall. Giant wheels help them to race over rocks and crush cars.

Top speed

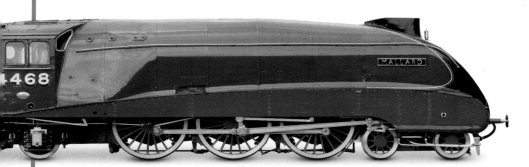

Mallard

In 1938, the British Mallard set a steam train speed record of 202 kph (125 mph). This record has never been broken.

X-15

This rocket-powered aircraft holds the speed record for a piloted plane. It reached 7,274 kph (4,519 mph).

Cockpit for one pilot

Westland Lynx

In 1986, this Westland Lynx set the record for fastest helicopter in the world. It flew at a speed of 400 kph (249 mph).

Spirit of Australia

No boat has travelled quicker on water than Spirit of Australia. It set a world record-breaking speed of 511 kph (317 mph) in 1978.

Engine is cooled by taking in air

Wooden hull

Pointed front helps boat go faster

Concorde

Concorde was the world's fastest passenger jet. It could travel at a speed of 2,179 kph (1,354 mph), more than twice the speed of sound.

The jet could carry 128 passengers

Movable nose was lowered for takeoff

Ack Attack

Inside this odd-shaped machine is the quickest motorcycle on the planet. It can travel as fast as a jet plane.

Bullet-nosed front section

Body made of carbon-fibre, which is a light but strong material

Bugatti Veyron

Reaching a top speed of 431 kph (267 mph), the Bugatti Veyron is the world's fastest mass-produced car. Only 450 cars were ever built.

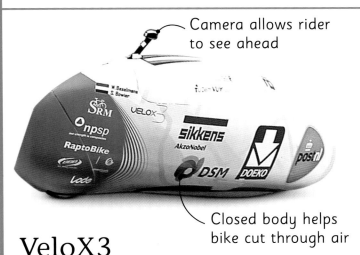

Camera allows rider to see ahead

Closed body helps bike cut through air

VeloX3

Built by a team of students from the Netherlands in 2013, this strange-looking vehicle is the world's fastest bicycle. It reached a speed of 134 kph (83 mph).

Vestas Sailrocket

The fastest sailing boat of all is the Vestas Sailrocket. In 2012, it used only wind power to reach an average speed of 121 kph (75 mph).

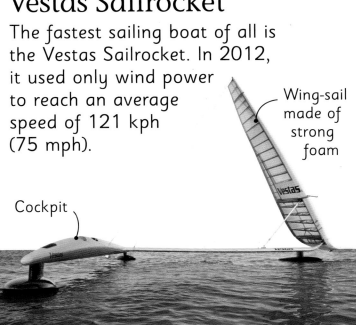

Wing-sail made of strong foam

Cockpit

Amazing machines

Giant wheel loader

This wheel loader is carrying a massive rock. The rock weighs almost as much as three large elephants!

Giant shovel

Harrier jump jet

The Harrier can rise straight up into the air. It is known as a VTOL jet, which stands for "vertical take-off and landing".

Nose cone

Wingtip wheel

Extreme motorbike

Built by Colin Furze, the longest motorbike in the world measures 14 m (46 ft) in length.

This motorbike can travel at a speed of 48 kph (30 mph)

Super stretch limousine

A super stretch limousine is a very long car. It has four windows running down each side.

The windows are tinted so that no one can see inside

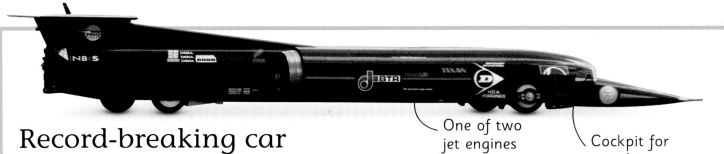

One of two jet engines

Cockpit for one driver

Record-breaking car

The fastest land vehicle in the world, the jet-powered Thrust SSC, set a world land speed record of 1,228 kph (763 mph) in 1997.

Juggernaut

This monster American juggernaut has 18 wheels. It is so heavy and makes such wide turns that it can only travel on main roads.

Space Shuttle

The Shuttle was the first spacecraft that could be used more than once. It had wings that helped it glide back to Earth.

Giant dump truck

If you stood next to this dump truck, you would only reach about halfway up one of the wheels. The truck is almost as tall as a house. It can carry enormous loads of waste away from a building site or quarry.

45

Up in space

Shuttle crawler

This is one of the largest land vehicles in the world. It is used to carry spacecraft, such as rockets and shuttles, to and from the launch pad.

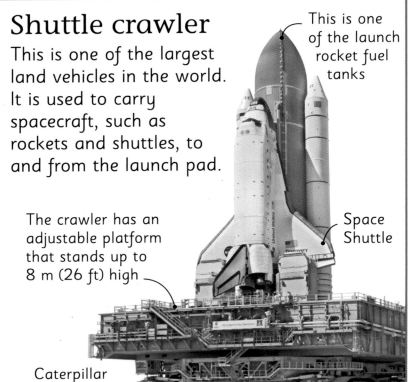

This is one of the launch rocket fuel tanks

The crawler has an adjustable platform that stands up to 8 m (26 ft) high

Space Shuttle

Caterpillar tracks

Lunar rover

When astronauts landed on the Moon, they moved around using a lunar rover. It was powered by a small battery.

Control unit to operate the rover

Rocket

Rockets are vehicles with powerful engines that can carry astronauts, spacecraft, and cargo into space. Saturn V was the world's tallest rocket, measuring 110 m (363 ft).

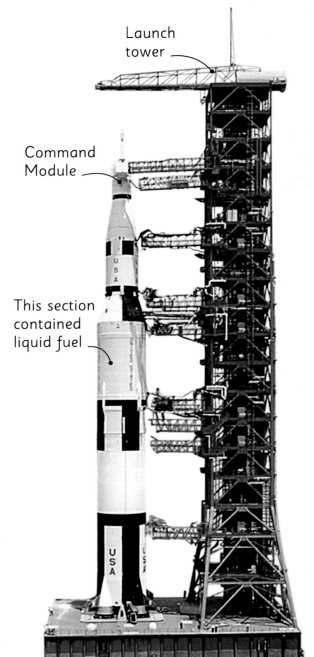

Launch tower

Command Module

This section contained liquid fuel

Cargo spacecraft

The Dragon is a modern spacecraft designed by the company SpaceX. It is used to carry cargo – and will eventually carry humans – to and from outer space.

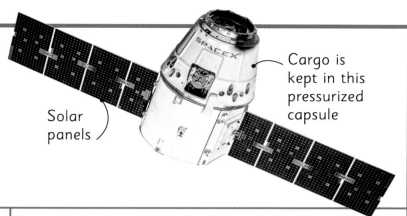

Cargo is kept in this pressurized capsule

Solar panels

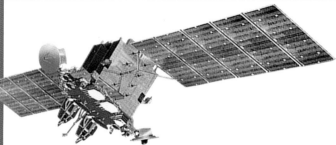

Satellite

Satellites, such as the AsiaSat 5, orbit around the Earth and provide signals for televisions, radios, and telephones.

Mars rover

This craft travels on the surface of Mars. It collects rock samples for research and takes pictures that are sent back to Earth.

Camera gives an all-round view of the planet's surface

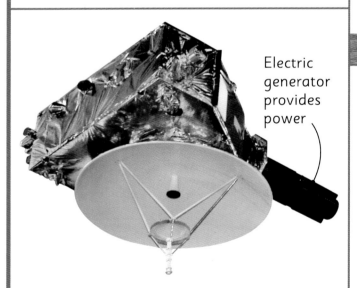

Electric generator provides power

Space probe

After travelling for nine years, New Horizons became the first space probe to explore the dwarf planet Pluto, in 2015.

Space station

Space stations are huge laboratories where astronauts can live and conduct research in space. The International Space Station is the largest one in operation today.

Index